Stop Smoking Through Self-Hypnosis

How to Order:

Quantity discounts are available from Prima Publishing & Communications, Post Office Box 1260SS, Rocklin, CA 95677; Telephone: (916) 624-5718. On your letterhead, include information concerning the intended use of the books and the number of books you wish to purchase.

U.S. Bookstores and Libraries: Please submit all orders to St. Martin's Press, 175 Fifth Avenue, New York, NY 10010. Telephone: (212) 674-5151.

Canadian Bookstores and Libraries: Please submit all orders to Raincoast Book Distribution, Ltd., 112 E. 3rd Ave., Vancouver, B.C., Canada, V5T IC8; Telephone: (604) 873-6581.

Stop Smoking Through Self-Hypnosis

Isabel Gilbert

FOR ORDER OR CATALOG
WESTWOOD PUBLISHING CO.
700 S. Central Avenue
Glendale CA 91204
(818) 242-1159

FOR ORDER OR CATALOG
WESTWOOD PUBLISHING CO.
700 S. Central Avenue
Glendale CA 91204
(818) 242-1159

Cover Design: Dunlavey Studios
Editor: Mary Peppers-Johnson
Typography: Ad Type Graphics

Library of Congress Cataloging-in-Publication Data
Gilbert, Isabel, 1917-
Stop smoking through self-hypnosis.

Previously published: The no smoking book.
Glendale, Calif. : Westwood Pub. Co., c1986.

Bibliography: p.
1. Tobacco habit. 2. Smoking. 3. Self-perception.
4. Autogenic training. I. Title.

HV5733.G54 1987   613.8'5   87-22568
ISBN 0-914629-36-0 (pbk.)

88 89 90 91   RRD   10 9 8 7 6 5 4 3 2 1

Printed in the United States of America

Every person has two educations,
that which is given to him
and that which he gives to himself.
What we are merely taught seldom
nourishes the mind like that
which we teach ourselves.

JEAN PAUL RICHTER
(1763-1825)

CONTENTS

FOREWORD

Books that are good for us are seldom much fun to read. *Stop Smoking Through Self-Hypnosis* is not only educational but also makes delightful reading.

People who smoke have usually been unconsciously hypnotized by misrepresentation of facts in advertisements. They begin to believe that cigarette smoking makes the smoker sophisticated, cool and relaxed, happy, athletic, rich, and capable of attracting friends and mates. Anyone who can remember his first experience with a cigarette will realize how important it has been for the tobacco industry to repeat such illusory suggestions. Now, a warning must be printed on every package of cigarettes. The wording of this suggests that one man, Luther L. Terry, M.D., "has determined" that smoking is dangerous to health. In 1964 the surgeon general of the United States credited more than 188 individuals and institutions who took part in the research that culminated in his report. He found that nicotine is only one part of the problem. The great heat at the end of a cigarette creates carcinogenic tars from innocuous substances in the tobacco leaf. Aldehydes, acids, and phenols irritate the mucus membranes, making them more vulnerable to long-range dangers.

Isabel Gilbert has done much research in formulating common-sense reasons to help the smoker kick the habit. A gifted hypnotherapist, with years of experience, she has taught the consciously willing but subconsciously resistant person to protect himself from terminating treatment or backtracking after a cure. Her ability to offer her ideas compellingly and amusingly comes from years of hard work as a professional writer.

It has been a privilege and a pleasure reading this book — but its message is serious. The person who follows the directions so artfully given here will gain not only a permanent victory over a dangerous habit but also a method of self-help that is much needed in this day of ever-increasing environmental threats to our health and happiness.

David B. Cheek, M.D.
San Francisco, California

ACKNOWLEDGMENTS

Or, Were It Not for You

This is a book of fact, not speculation; a book of "how to," not a pep talk; a book of "you can," not "you should." In part, it is a report on knowledge derived from my years of experience working with addicted smokers; and, in part, as all factual books are, it is a restatement of the knowledge of experts in the field of medicine and psychology, and of information acquired from experiences documented in medical journals.

Among my teachers, I want to acknowledge with special appreciation the work of David B. Cheek, M.D., whose hypnosis training workshops, lectures, and discussions helped me formulate many of the ideas in this book. Personal thanks go to the memory of my dear friend, Miriam Allen de Ford, whose encouraging words kept me at the typewriter. I appreciate, too, Anne M. Schmid of the University of California, San Francisco, for her assistance in researching the medical information. And, an extra thank-you goes to my friend Gloria North for her sustained emotional support and optimism.

INTRODUCTION

Or, Warming Up to the Effort

Chant the following, murmuring or out loud, to yourself. Repeat it s-l-o-w-l-y until you feel your decision-making muscles begin to flex.

I HAVE ONLY ONE LIFE AND ONE BODY.
I NEED MY BODY TO LIVE.
SMOKING IS POISON TO MY BODY.

(Pause)

I WAS NOT BORN SMOKING;
I CHOSE TO SMOKE.
NOW I CHOOSE *NOT* TO SMOKE

Chapter 1

The Teaser
Or, Waiting for Godot?

(Read this
before
you skim)

> A good intention clothes itself with power.
> RALPH WALDO EMERSON

No, you were not born smoking. You chose to smoke* and continue to smoke, for reasons we will examine later. But you are the only one who can change, and that's what this book is all about.

Don't skim through, though, looking for a magic cure. There is none — no magic pill or wand, no prayer wheel, no amulet or talisman that will suddenly remove your addiction. But there is a way to become a permanent *non*smoker. It is an easier and less painful way than that of grinding self-denial. It can be done through relaxation and imagination — by developing a new attitude toward your smoking, toward yourself, and toward your life. Thousands of people have done it, and you, too, can conquer your addiction without the slightest difficulty.

IMPORTANT — It's up to you. You will be working with your own brain — re-educating it — working with your own nervous system — retraining it — to reverse a self-destructive habit. You are your own guru.

WARNING — You may start working on the techniques outlined here, then drop out somewhere along the way. Of course, nothing will change. You may be one who will almost make it. The "almoster" is the person who starts a project, and, just when success is imminent, perversely gives up.

---

*The word *smoke* refers to cigarettes, cigars, or pipes.

BUT — If you are serious about quitting smoking and are willing to practice these techniques ONE DAY AT A TIME, you will definitely succeed. I call them *heightened awareness techniques,* which seem to me more descriptive than *self-hypnosis,* another appropriate term.

Chapter 2

Motivation
Or, The Trade-Off

(Nobody really wants to quit smoking)

How do I know what I think
until I hear what I have to say?
LEWIS CARROLL

Nobody really wants to quit smoking. But if you want to want, you are a candidate for this easy method of doing so. You can talk yourself into quitting. You can inspire your mind with the definite decision and then take action. Your decision to quit ingesting nicotine is a decision to live — to live longer and to make your life healthier, cleaner, and happier.

Doctors claim that the life span is increased many years when you quit smoking. You have clean, healthy lungs, more energy, more wind, and better general health. Esthetically, your mouth is fresher; your breath, sweeter. Also, you'll certainly have more cash in your pocket.

Decision-making muscles still stiff?

You've been toying with the decision to quit smoking for a long time. Now, you are ready. Make sure that you are not deciding because a wife, a husband, or a friend has goaded you to stop smoking. You are taking this step for only one person, *yourself.*

What you are doing is making a trade. You are giving up smoking for a longer life — a trade *all in your favor.* The realization that you are breaking an addiction brings an upsurge of new confidence that carries over to all areas of your life.

Now, let's examine some gruesome scientific facts that will accentuate your wise decision to quit smoking.

Nicotine is lethal. Whether you are smoking cigarettes, cigars, or pipes, you are ingesting nicotine poison and other injurious substances. More specifically, this is what happens: When heat combines with tobacco, it distills a new and dangerous substance called *coal tar,* which damages the tissue of any organ in the body it touches. Additionally, small amounts of carbon monoxide and arsenic are present in tobacco smoke.

Scientific researchers report that the nicotine (plus other substances in tobacco) is absorbed by and accumulates in the body when smoke is inhaled. Also, some of the poisons are absorbed when smoke is puffed without inhaling.

Chapter 3

Scientific Facts
Or, Doctors Tell It Like It Is

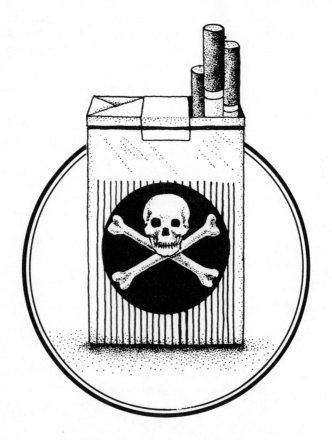

(The gruesome details)

Men do not usually die;
they kill themselves.
MICHEL DE MONTAIGNE

When you quit smoking, you are not giving up pleasure. You are giving up poison. The poison you are rejecting is nicotine. Scientists consider nicotine one of the most dangerous poisons in existence. If a person ingested a quantity of concentrated nicotine equal to one week's smoking of a pack of cigarettes a day, he would die.

You scoff. How come, you ask, so many smokers are still living and puffing away?

Fortunately, the smoker does not absorb all the nicotine from one smoke. Some of it is lost at the mouth; some is dispersed through the body; and perhaps only one-tenth of the nicotine from each puff enters the blood stream. Still, when you multiply this by sixty smokes a day, the body is bound to retain a good deal of the poison.

The human body is a fantastic instrument because it protects itself for survival. During sleep, the body's immune mechanism helps a smoker eliminate some of the nicotine poison, thus preventing the buildup of a lethal dose. This does not whitewash the dangers of smoking. On the contrary, it only explains why such deadly poison hasn't killed the smoker instantly.

The effects of smoking are believed to be cumulative. That is, although the body builds up a tolerance to the *immediate* effects of the poisonous nicotine, that very tolerance permits continued ingestion of the smoke, which, over a period of time, has a debilitating effect on almost every area of the body.

Millions of people quit smoking *before* their body organs and functions break down. If, unfortunately, you already have a serious illness, such as heart or lung trouble, high blood pressure, emphysema, or other physical problems, you can arrest or sometimes completely eliminate the disease, and certainly improve your general health, by stopping smoking.

Lung cancer, the most publicized tobacco villain, is not the only illness a smoker has to fear. Researchers have conclusively linked many other physical disorders to nicotine deposits in the body.

According to Alton Ochsner, M.D., in an article in *American Scientist,* "The use of tobacco is hazardous because it produces cancer, vascular deterioration, pulmonary disease, reproductive disorders, ulcers, disabling illness and premature deaths, and tremendous economic loss."[1] Let's examine some of these diseases.

Smoking and Your Heart

For years cardiologists have warned their patients about the adverse effects of smoking. No one with coronary heart disease should incur added risk to his heart by smoking. Whether your heart is diseased or healthy, smoking takes its toll. The Tobacco Heart, described by cardiologists when a patient complains of chest pains, irregular beats, dizziness, and shortness of breath, has been clearly demonstrated to be caused by smoking. Often these symptoms disappear completely when the patient quits smoking.

Buerger's Disease

Buerger's disease is caused when circulation to the extremities is disrupted. The extremities become numb, and the affected areas show blotches of dead tissue that break down further, resulting in serious consequences. This circulatory disease is certainly related to smoking. Tobacco constricts the blood vessels and inhibits the flow of blood, particularly through the smaller vessels.

Johnny A. Blue, M.D., F.A.C., in an article in *Annals of Allergy,* points out, "It is well known today that tobacco has a peculiar affinity for blood vessels. Another evidence of tobacco allergy is that thromboangitis obliterans does not occur after the patient stops smoking."[2]

Respiratory Ailments and Allergy

Of course, everyone is familiar with the smoker's hack; television and other media have brought this to our attention. Lung cancer, emphysema, bronchitis, asthma, tuberculosis, and all breakdowns of lung tissue have been irrevocably connected to smoking.

In the previously mentioned article, Blue states, "It is also well recognized that 'smoker's asthma,' which simulates allergic bronchial asthma, disappears when the patient stops smoking." He cites the work of Rosen and Levy, who described the case of an infant whose asthma attacks were promptly relieved when the parents stopped smoking and were reproduced when the parents resumed smoking. This demonstrates that nicotine inhaled from the atmosphere (not directly from a smoke) can still be poisonous. Blue concludes that "smoking has a triple effect in that it reacts pharmacologically, as an allergen, and as a local irritant."

Leading laryngologists have noted that the secretion of mucus in the nasal pharynx is affected by a single puff of an average-size cigarette. The vocal cords, or the larynx, develop anything from mild infection, to tumors, to loss of voice.

According to Ochsner, "The incidence of pulmonary emphysema is increasing rapidly, and the severe form is almost invariably the result of smoking, particularly cigarettes."

What about your stomach? Gastroenterologists say that the tar in cigarettes irritates the gastric lining of the stomach and depresses the nerve endings which increase gastric secretion and activity. The tar dissolved in the sputum becomes an irritant and depresses the appetite.

How about surgical risks? Anesthesiologists bemoan surgical patients who smoke heavily. It has been established that smokers are more difficult to anesthetize than nonsmokers.[3] Further, smokers often develop a laryngeal spasm when administered anesthetics such as ether. Such constriction could prove fatal. All anesthesiologists agree that any person contemplating surgery should stop smoking a long time prior to the procedure.

Let's Examine the Nerves

"There's nothing like a cigarette to calm my jumpy nerves!" is the typical smoker's refrain.

Wrong! Such claims have been programmed into his mind by advertising that portrays people in nerve-wracking situations reaching for a smoke to ease their anxieties. The smoker subconsciously accepts these obviously planted suggestions and incorporates them into his own inner program.

A neurologist researched the effects of smoking on finger tremors. Using an instrument called the tronometer, he measured smokers' finger tremors before and after they smoked. After only one cigarette, regular smokers' tremors increased 39 percent. Nonsmokers who did not inhale registered no change. Nonsmokers who did inhale registered an 82 percent increase in finger tremors after one cigarette.

That isn't all. Disturbances of the kidneys, the pancreas, and even the reproductive organs can be related to smoking. According to Ochsner, it has been demonstrated that mothers who smoke have a greater number of premature and low birth-weight babies than those who do not. He concludes that upon cessation of smoking, "an accession of high spirits, energy, appetite and sexual potency . . . make the chief symptoms of tobacco smoking plain."

According to Travis E. Solomon and Dr. Eugene D. Jacobson, "In human subjects who have smoked more than one package of cigarettes per day for more than three years, the pancreatic output of bicarbonates (as measured by the double secretin test) is chronically depressed as compared with the nonsmokers."[3] Conditions of the pancreas have been known to improve or have been eradicated when a patient quits smoking.

Smoking and Ulcers

Authors Solomon and Jacobson also note, "The use of tobacco is harmful to patients with peptic and duodenal ulcer . . . [we are] convinced that patients with ulcers cannot be cured as long as they smoke."

A Fuzzy World and Other Annoyances

According to ophthalmologists, smoking definitely attenuates the sense of vision. Doctors say that optic neuritis, night blindness, dilated pupils, and inability to focus are consequences of heavy smoking. An article in the December 1955 *Virginia Medical Monthly* states that examinations by ophthalmologists demonstrated that after a smoker had two cigarettes, his optic nerve showed a grayish outline, a dullness, and a gradual paralysis of his entire optic disc.

How many smokers do you think would continue smoking if each cigarette brought on the acute reaction from nicotine poisoning sometimes experienced by a new smoker: nausea, vomiting, cramps, blurred vision, and diarrhea? Whatever his original motive for smoking, the smoker continues to build up tolerance with each cigarette he inhales, and his body's negative reactions decrease as the cells adjust. Soon, the smoker is addicted and all memory of the first miserable jolt is obliterated.

Occasionally, even heavy smokers experience the above negative symptoms plus a progressive cough, sinus congestion, and postnasal drip — all minor ills compared to the serious troubles cited earlier. They usually disregard these annoying but not incapacitating ailments, or excuse them by attributing them to causes other than smoking. However, nose specialists say that postnasal drip and sinusitis often diminish and sometimes disappear when heavy smokers with these problems quit completely.

Have you cut down smoking? Good. Naturally, decreasing the nicotine poison in your system helps. But even if you've cut down to one or two smokes a day, you are still ingesting nicotine.

The "kick" or lift from the smoke you feel occurs only when the nicotine poison enters your tissues. Without the nicotine, a cigarette would be as stimulating as if it were filled with orange peel. As long as you are smoking even one cigarette, the body cells continue to be activated by the poison. You are merely controlling the number of smokes. In time, people who cut down this way invariably find themselves back to their former frequency, or pretty close to it. You may cut down, then build up again under stress, repeating the performance like a yo-yo, up and down, up and down.

Take the case of Ellen M., a twenty-eight-year-old mother of two and a former smoker of two and one-half packs of cigarettes a day, who developed a morning cough that progressed to chronic bronchitis. Her doctor insisted that she quit smoking. Instead of quitting, she worked hard at control and reduced her smoking to one pack a day. The bronchitis subsided and Ellen, a skier, made a decision. She would take a two-week skiing vacation — you can't smoke while skiing! She enjoyed the two weeks and reduced her smoking to two cigarettes per day.

Very proud of her achievement, she returned home to her usual environment and old behavior patterns. Within three months (with great effort to control the smoking), Ellen was back to her two-and-one-half-packs-a-day schedule — and her cough and bronchitis were back also.

Controlling your smoking merely denies the cells the nicotine they demand. Besides being a nervous strain, controlling keeps the cells agitated and sustains your addiction.

Finally, Ellen made a firm decision to stop playing the yo-yo game — to quit completely. She did this by using heightened awareness techniques. Within weeks, all her symptoms cleared up, and for more than a year, Ellen has remained a nonsmoker, enjoying her newly attained healthy condition. When I congratulated her, Ellen said, "Nothing and nobody could ever make me take that first smoke."

In my twelve years of experience helping smokers quit by heightened awareness training, I have found that cutting down smoking (while salutary, of course) simply sustains addiction.

Two- or three-pack smokers who have cut down to the last five cigarettes find it just as difficult to relinquish the few as they do to stop abruptly.

The cutoff must be like a surgical removal: complete and permanent. You can do this without a withdrawal jolt to the nervous system by using relaxation techniques. Since you smoke when you feel tense, you can quit smoking easily by relaxing and releasing tension, thereby removing the reason for a smoke. The heightened awareness techniques in this book have been designed for this purpose.

Chapter 4

A Tragic Soliloquy

Or, I Try Harder

(Stop trying so hard)

Full of sound and fury, signifying nothing.
SHAKESPEARE

Ah, but I've done it so many times! Quit, I mean,
like the man who said, "I've lost the same five pounds
hundreds of times." The times include a day,
a month; once, even a year. But . . . well, see
this cigarette here?

My ploys have been classic — not buying, then bumming;
alternating cigars, pipes, and inferior-tasting brands.
(Even now, see my hand,
without an order from my conscious mind,
grope for a smoke?)

But I weary of the damn stale smell
that comes from every ashtray
placed so well in every room.
And, God! My tongue!

I punctuate my most profound comments with rattling
coughs. And, forsooth, my early morning bed groans,
not from love,
but from snorts and gurgles as I struggle
to clear my nose and lungs.

Will power? My family, rightly so I guess,
says I have none.
In truth, I'm getting scared!

I shall try again with firm resolve.
Grind on!
(Ah, tight my jaw. And teeth?
My fists are clenched, my shoulders hunched,
and nerve ends whine.)

I want a smoke!

Is this some sort of joke?
The more I try, the more I feel the yoke.
This just can't be the way at all.
Gadzooks, it's not the way at all!

So, stop trying to stop. A conscious determination to quit smoking builds inner conflict. One part of your mind says, "I will quit, I must quit, I have to quit." Another part of your mind says, "But I don't really want to quit." The battle is on. The two opposing forces vie for supremacy. With the first moment of pressure, strong emotion, or sudden excitement, the older, stronger pattern conquers the new, younger one. Back you swing to the established way.

This sets into action the law of reversed effort. It is like the new bicycle rider wobbling along who suddenly sees a huge rock and is determined to miss it. By focusing intently on the rock, he invariably runs right into it.

Another example, perhaps more common: Have you ever tried to remember a name? You try hard. You strain the memory but you cannot think of it. Then later, when you've stopped trying, the name springs spontaneously into the mind.

Zealous or overzealous resolve not only defeats your goal but actually attracts its opposite. The trick is to let go, hang loose. *Don't try to make anything happen.* Open your mind to the new thought and allow it to happen to you.

Chapter 5

As The Commercial Turns

Or, How to End Up on Top

(Nag, nag, nag)

Nothing succeeds like success.
ALEXANDRE DUMAS (pere)

A Scenario for Television

THE CAST

OUTER JOE, *a forty-two-year-old advertising executive; father of three; and two-pack-a-day smoker.*

INNER JOE, *his constant companion*

UNDERSTUDIES, *any smoker*

Act I

The time is an early morning in January. The place is a prosperous house in the suburbs where OUTER JOE, his family, and INNER JOE live. [Fade-in]
The scene opens with a long shot of Joe's bedroom and shows the entrance to his dressing room and bathroom. The camera pans to a close-up of OUTER JOE in bed, his hand groping for cigarettes on a night table. He hacks a couple of times before lighting up a cigarette, then is able to control

*himself long enough to take a shallow drag, as he swings his
legs over the edge of the bed onto the floor. He continues
hacking.*

INNER JOE: Gee, Joe, it's really great waking up with you in
the morning! A real experience, it is. Reminds me of the
good old days in our wet, freezing bunker in Korea . . . ya
know, when we all had the flu?

OUTER JOE: *[Between puffs and hacks]* Knock it off! You're
beginning to sound like my wife . . . and my secretary . . .
and like *[Pause]* well, like everybody I know.

INNER JOE: *Me* knock it off! Why the hell don't *you?* The old
coffin tacks *[Chuckle],* I mean.

OUTER JOE: *[Moving to bathroom as camera follows]* I will
. . . I will. Gonna quit on my vacation in July. I'll have time
to think about it.

INNER JOE: You said that last year . . . about vacation and
quitting.

*The camera shows a close-up of Joe's hands, fading in, as he
places a cigarette in an ashtray on top of the toilet shelf. He
knocks the cigarette into the toilet bowl and reaches for
another.*

OUTER JOE: Damn! *[Puff, puff]* I really should quit . . . it's a
killer. *[Puffs, coughs, and spits into toilet.]*

INNER JOE: Man, you're really beautiful in the morning — ugh!
Anybody with any sense sure wouldn't want to greet the old
morning sun with *you.*

OUTER JOE: Cut the nagging. I know I should quit.

INNER JOE: So why don't you? Like today?

OUTER JOE: *[Mumbling as he brushes his teeth]* No, not today.
Joe Junior starts school. Too much excitement.

INNER JOE: Cop out! Just a cop out!

OUTER JOE: Yeah? Think so? *[Contemplatively]* Okay, right
now. Watch me! *[He throws a package of cigarettes into the
wastebasket, looks at his teeth in the mirror, and grimaces,*

shaking his head in disgust. He then assumes a confident look.]

INNER JOE: Atta way!

[Fade-out]

[Fade-in, Joe's family room]

    JOE is walking toward a ringing telephone where a pack of cigarettes, matches, and an ashtray lie. He picks up the phone and cradles it between his shoulders and ear while he fumbles for and lights a cigarette. He seems aware only of the voice at the other end.

[Fade-out]

[Fade-in, JOE leaving house puffing a cigarette]

INNER JOE: Hey, fella! Thought you quit back there!

OUTER JOE: Oh, uh . . . well, that damned client. Impossible deadline . . . wants a complete new spring advertising campaign, fresh approach, all that and only two weeks . . . oh boy.

INNER JOE: That's right, Joe. When you're uptight, get yourself a little poison.

OUTER JOE: Don't be an ass. *[Contemplating]* I'll get it done.

INNER JOE: I said, d'ya have to poison yourself?

OUTER JOE: What d'ya mean? You're crazy today!

INNER JOE: Look, man. You read the surgeon general's report. Nicotine is poison; so ya get nervous and poison yourself. There!

OUTER JOE: I've got other things on my mind. Shut up!

INNER JOE: Okay, I will.

[Fade-out. JOE stomps out puffing]

Act II

The time is a year later; the place, Joe's family room.
[Fade-in]

The scene opens with a close-up of JOE reading the paper and watching television. Next to him is an ashtray loaded with cigarette butts and another holding a charred pipe and cigar butts. He glances at both with disgust, shrugs, and continues to read the paper. The camera shows a close-up of the paper's headline: LUNG CANCER CLAIMS JET-SET PACESETTER.

OUTER JOE: *[Contemplatively]* Hmmm . . . two packs a day. Well, I do have *something* in common with the Jet Set.

INNER JOE: *[Sarcastically]* Quite an accomplishment.

OUTER JOE: Well, maybe I should quit . . . uh . . . again?

INNER JOE: Yeah, while you're still around and breathing!

OUTER JOE: Aw, come on. Nothing wrong with my lungs. Last month's physical . . .

INNER JOE: *[Interrupting]* Nothing wrong *yet!* Remember, even the surgeon general warns that smoking is dangerous to your health.

OUTER JOE: *[Face lighting up]* Exercise! That's what I need. I'll start jogging every morning before work.

INNER JOE: You're stubborn, Joe! Impossible!

OUTER JOE: Look, I just don't have time to think about it now.

[Fade-out]

[Fade-in]

The camera shows a montage of JOE jogging, gasping for breath, and sweating heavily; JOE changing from a sweat suit to a business suit, with a cigarette in his mouth; JOE at his dinner table, extinguishing a cigarette butt in a saucer; JOE at his office, blowing smoke in a young female art director's face while reviewing a layout.

[Fade-out]

ACT III

The time is two years later in the late afternoon; the place, Joe's office. JOE now smokes three packs a day.

The scene opens with a full camera view of JOE, obviously upset, standing by his desk and talking on the phone.

OUTER JOE: Hi, honey! Glad I could catch you. *[Pause]* No, I'm all right. It's Harry. *[Pause]* Heart attack. *[Pause]* Yeah, I'm going right over. *[Pause]* No, they think he'll make it. What? *[Pause]* But guess things will really change now. Well, you know . . . that Harry . . . pressure, hard work, and . . . well, you know. He always had his head in a hazy cloud of smoke. *[Pause]* Okay. See you soon as I can. Love you. *[Hangs up]*

INNER JOE: Okay, Mister Put It Off. Let's face some facts!

OUTER JOE: Right! Right! This is not some far-off celebrity. This is my boss, my friend, my mentor. Gee . . . really rocks you.

INNER JOE: Soooo?

OUTER JOE: I know, I know! Harry has to stop smoking immediately. *[Hesitates]* And, I guess I should too.

INNER JOE: So?

The camera follows JOE as he scoops up all of his smoking paraphernalia.

[Fade-out]

[Fade-in]

The camera shows a close-up of Joe's hand flushing a toilet and the remains of his habit swirling around in the bowl, then disappearing.

Appearing next is a montage of JOE snarling at his wife; JOE snarling at his secretary; JOE snarling at a cab driver; JOE chewing gum; JOE popping lifesavers into his mouth; JOE gazing longingly at a smoke shop; JOE stepping on a scale.

[Fade-out]

Act IV

It is two weeks later in the late evening.
[Fade-in]
The scene opens with a long shot of Joe's family room;
JOE is pacing the floor.

OUTER JOE: This is nuts!

INNER JOE: You're doing great! Just hold on, brother.

OUTER JOE: Hold on to what? *[Frantically, he searches the drawers of the side tables, finds a limp, dirty cigarette in the trash can, and lights it up with a sigh of relief.]*

INNER JOE: *[Disgustedly]* Ya just blew it! Why the . . .

OUTER JOE: Nag, nag, nag. You, my wife, my secretary . . . everybody. You think you . . . they . . . have won? No way! I put up with a hell of a lot, make a lot of concessions . . . listen to people tell me what to do! This is one damn place where I'm boss!

INNER JOE: Are you? Or are you just getting even?

OUTER JOE: Whatever . . . yes, you bet! And it feels good!

INNER JOE: *[Disgustedly]* What a dope! You think you're punishing the naggers? Dope. You're just punishing yourself.

OUTER JOE: *[Vaguely]* Well . . . but look! I'm sure not unique. *[The rest of the dialogue is rapid and interruptive.]* The TV doctor smokes before surgery . . . nerves . . .

INNER JOE: Propaganda . . . a commercial. You should know . . .

OUTER JOE: . . . and look at that triumphant, grime-streaked driver who climbs out of his winning XKG! He lights up . . .

INNER JOE: . . . you should know! Another commercial!

OUTER JOE: . . . and the performer who takes that last, long drag before facing the footlights . . .

INNER JOE: Aw, come on . . . suggestion . . . pure suggestion. Almost subliminal, bombarded by images that are really *selling* you something . . . or an idea . . . or an accepted way of acting, especially under stress! And suggestion is your busi . . .

OUTER JOE: Okay, okay, okay . . . and suggestion *is* my business! So, why don't I work up a suggestion for myself? Huh?

INNER JOE: Yeah . . . atta boy! Brilliant. Brains plus!

OUTER JOE: Just because you win, don't get smart! *[Pause]* Hmmm. A commercial for Joe! I like the idea.

INNER JOE: Atta boy . . .

OUTER JOE: *[Contemplating, snaps fingers]* I have it. Here's the scenario. Try it on for size: A full-front scene of a man, about forty-two, healthy and vigorous looking. Then, a montage of man: swatting a tennis ball; dancing under moonlight; a close-up of a tense business conversation.

VOICE OVER: I'm a permanent nonsmoker. I no longer need that crutch. And this time I make it stick.

INNER JOE: You're a genius, Joe. No wonder Harry chose you to take his place!

TITLE BOARD AND VOICE OVER: *I'm a permanent nonsmoker. I no longer need that crutch. And this time I make it stick.*

INNER JOE: *[Voice fading]* Hey! Joe, now that you're on your own, you don't need me anymore. Heyyyyyyyyyyyyyy.

Chapter 6

Lamentations
Or, It Only Hurts
When I Laugh

(The old withdrawal symptoms)

It is much easier to suppress a
first desire than to satisfy
those that follow.
ROCHEFOUCAULD

Withdrawal symptoms vary in kind and intensity and depend upon many factors: how long you have smoked; how much you have smoked; your general health and the state of your nervous system; and how high-strung and emotional you are. Every human being is different. The more years and the more smoking, the more loaded your cells are with nicotine poison. Ergo, the more you will have to work.

The one-pack-a-day smoker may find it easier than the three-pack smoker, but this is not always true. Regardless of your category, you can rise above any discomfort and ride over the moments of craving using heightened awareness techniques.

Withdrawal symptoms are psychological and physiological and often surprising. Take the case of Ralph T., a forty-year-old salesman and two-pack-a-day smoker, who decided to quit before the birth of his first child. From the first nonsmoking day, using his heightened awareness techniques, Ralph lost absolutely all desire to smoke. Although he was under constant tension, he had no physiological withdrawal symptoms. None whatsoever. Perhaps the motivation was exceptionally powerful. He wanted to live to see his child (a son) grow up to manhood with a healthy father.

On the other hand, Elaine P., forty-two and a mother of three, was a chronic worrier with a strong "poor me" psychology.

Although she had smoked barely one pack a day, she found quitting more difficult. Anxiety was a built-in part of her makeup. If she didn't have something tangible to worry about, she created it.

Even Elaine, however, conquered by riding over the short periods of craving, learning to live her life one day at a time with relaxation. In her case, the quit-smoking heightened awareness techniques carried over into all areas of her life and became a tool for a more relaxed, more enjoyable attitude toward herself and her family.

Still another baffling case was Toni W., the wife of a busy doctor, responsible for running a large house and raising four small children. She smoked one and one-half packs a day and decided to quit just before Christmas. I urged her to wait until after the holidays, especially since she admitted to a heavy social schedule and expected visiting relatives. But Toni insisted, saying, "If I wait for a quiet time in my life, I'll never do it. This is no more hectic than any other time." Here was another surprise. Toni quit and, using her heightened awareness techniques, did not have one moment of disquiet. She breezed through a very exciting, busy holiday season, giving and attending parties where people all around her smoked, but she had no desire to.

What about being deprived of the oral satisfaction of popping objects into your mouth — cigarettes, pipes, and cigars? Rightly or wrongly, you have connected this action with pleasure. You've quit smoking; so what happens to this artificial need for gratifying oral stimulation? Can you cope with the fact that now your taste buds are clean and are sending strong "delicious" signals to your brain? Now you can rediscover wonder and pleasure in food.

You *should* satisfy oral need, for denial builds old conflicts and makes you revert to trying too hard. You can satisfy this need by drinking a low-calorie carbonated soda, by chewing gum, by eating protein chewables, or by sucking a hard, sugarless candy. Even a drink of water will give you the satisfaction you need.

Remember, you need not gain weight when you quit smoking.

Naturally, if to satisfy oral need, you feast on chocolate, pastry, or other desserts, you certainly will gain weight. However, you can use the same techniques to ride over the craving for rich and fattening foods that you are using to defeat the craving for a smoke. But, think of the advantages if you are one who has been cursed with a poor appetite and has always been underweight.

A most important thing to remember while going through the withdrawal period is, *the body cells remember*. With just one smoke, the old addiction is reactivated. The cells say, "Wow, welcome back!" to the nicotine, and they are back in business with the craving. The demand and the poison return to plague your body and mind.

One man, a contractor-builder who had been a three-pack-a-day smoker, quit to his surprise, without difficulty. Within two weeks, his heavy cough and bronchitis cleared up. Each day he felt better. After several months of feeling strong and healthy again, he began to toy with the idea of taking just one cigarette. Just one. He did, and he smoked it. Nothing happened. He didn't feel that he must smoke more. He felt he had gotten away with it without the slightest ill effects and was quite smug about his performance. His heightened awareness techniques lapsed and finally dropped completely.

Several days later, he decided to try another cigarette. Again, he enjoyed it and did not feel a compulsion to continue. He felt more and more cocky, the old I-can-take-it-or-leave-it syndrome. The following week, he smoked two cigarettes within one day. Still no compulsive feelings.

I am sure you can guess how this story ended. Within two months he was back to his three-pack-a-day habit, and he had to go through the withdrawal period all over again after repeating the how-to-quit instructions.

Why punish yourself this way? *Remember, the cells remember*.

Chapter 7

The Three Stooges
Or, Who's in Charge?

(As if you didn't know)

> . . . and when we think we lead,
> we are most led.
> LORD BYRON

Later, we'll consider why you started smoking, or, rather, why you took your first smoke. Now, let's consider what keeps you smoking, a much more important consideration when it comes to quitting. What causes an action that *you don't want,* and how do *you* become boss? The three stooges playing boss are reflex habit, physiological need, and psychological need. Let's look at how these puppeteers pull the strings.

THE REFLEX HABIT

Cocktail?.................................... Cigarette

Great meal! .... Cigar

Coffee/tea/milk?.............................. Smoke

Telephone call................................ Light up

Evening news .... Pipe

And so it goes, the classic conditioned reflex response. You have programmed yourself well; stimulus equals automatic response, a robot, unaware. You are not thinking about the smoke, just doing it, reacting to a given situation as you have reacted many times to a previous similar experience, making it a fixed "mental set." Pavlov's dogs.

Physiological Need

Your body cells are addicted to nicotine. They demand the poison and set up an urge and a craving that only a smoke can satisfy. You become hooked. Face it, hooked just like the dope addict. Yep, that's you!

As mentioned earlier in the section on withdrawal symptoms, addicted cells need to be completely deprived of the poison, ventilated and renovated, until they quiet down and no longer crave. This is simply a matter of time. *You* provide this time by exercising your relaxation techniques and riding over the few seconds of craving during your first *non*smoking days until this stooge is in his proper place.

Psychological Need

The powerful emotions! If you're angry or excited, the smoke becomes a tranquilizer. If you're nervous, frustrated, or insecure, the smoke gives a (false) feeling of well-being and security.

You've done a good job? Have a (smoke) reward!

Everything is going wrong? Let's avoid it for a minute with a smoke.

Stymied in a creative endeavor? Pace and puff, waiting for the breakthrough.

What are we doing here? When upset, frustrated, stymied, or angry, would you say to yourself rationally, "I think I'll take a little poison"? Or, if you completed a task satisfactorily, would you want to reward yourself with the same poison?

In reality, a piece of paper filled with tobacco can in no way be considered a tranquilizer, a security blanket, or a reward. In your mind, however, you have identified the smoke with these feelings, and you are programmed to associate the effects of the poison with the gratification of needs. Silly? Yes, indeed.

Your constant association of the smoke with these emotions has created the need. Actually, it is not only an artificially created need, but a self-destructive one that you have associated with release of tension. The heightened awareness techniques are especially designed to meet the real need — release of tension — and thus replace the reason for smoking.

Repressed feelings are always given as reasons for smoking. You are angry. You disagree. Or, you don't like someone's action or speech. But you keep silent. Instead of responding, you smoke to alleviate your emotional turmoil. These conflicts build and require more smoking to drown more resentments and more conflicts, and perhaps more hate . . . even self-hate.

When you identify smoking with soothing disturbed emotions, you are doing two harmful things. You are repressing your own feelings, and you are not letting others know where they stand or what you think. You are not leveling with yourself or with others.

Why not level? Touch base with your feelings and thoughts. Speak out spontaneously without fear of consequence, without fear of what anyone will say or think. This doesn't mean that you have to be belligerent, violent, or nasty. You can say what you feel and what you think in a quiet voice and with a smile. It's more powerful and effective this way. A philosopher said, "The greatest sin in the world is to be dishonest with yourself." Polonius advised Hamlet, "To thine own self be true, and it must follow, as the night the day, thou canst not then be false to any man."

Emotional factors vary and can be quite complicated. What started as an innocent experiment becomes an addiction. For some, this addiction can be used as self-punishment. People with overdeveloped consciences ingest nicotine poison to punish themselves because of guilt feelings, either real or imagined. Perfectionists who expect too much of themselves sometimes subconsciously feel they deserve punishment.

Who's perfect? Since perfection is impossible, why not give yourself permission NOT TO BE PERFECT. Consider all your experiences, negative or positive, as learning processes that move you forward on the path of self-development and growth.

There is no need to suffer. Self-punishment exists only because you have chosen to punish yourself. Resentments only hurt the person who feels resentful. As Confucius said, "To be wrong is nothing unless you continue to remember it." You can decide to forgive. Forgive everyone, especially yourself. Be free of smoking and be free of guilt.

Your decision to quit smoking can be the harbinger of a new life, the first step on a path of self-renewal of body and mind, and an indication of growth and maturity.

Chapter 8

Mobilization
Or, Separation Blues

(Basic training, advanced maneuvers,
and psychological infiltration)

> Nothing great was ever
> achieved without enthusiasm.
> RALPH WALDO EMERSON

Preparing for the Liberation:
That First Nonsmoking Day

First, choose a specific date for the cutoff, about ten days to two weeks ahead. Choose a day that promises to be comparatively quiet, perhaps a weekend if weekends are your free days, or any other day when your life is easier. Mark that day on your calendar. Mark it boldly, perhaps in red, signifying that it will be a red-letter day in your life. During this period, you will be working toward breaking your reflex habits. Later, you will learn the techniques of heightened awareness which will allow you to control the psychological and physiological needs that perpetuate your addiction.

Basic Training — Breaking the Reflex Habits

THERE WILL BE NO UNCONSCIOUS, AUTOMATIC SMOKES. You must be aware of every smoke you light. Therefore:

1. Change brands of cigarettes, cigars, and/or pipe tobacco to something you like least.

2. Every time you light a cigarette, you are to think, "Now I'm lighting a cigarette, and I am going to smoke it." However, if you catch yourself puffing and do not remember doing it or having thought the statement, put out the cigarette and light it all over again.

3. As you become aware of each cigarette you light, delay the action. When you think of smoking, tell yourself, "Yes, I'm going to smoke, but not right now." Then distract your mind into other channels that will totally absorb your thoughts. Use your head. Divert your attention to another project, and do it with intensity.

Delay-distract — distract-delay. You will be cutting down and, at the same time, short-circuiting those deeply grooved reflexes. You can, if you wish, strengthen this delay tactic by suggesting to yourself before retiring, "Tomorrow I will not smoke until noon (or whatever time you choose)." The subconscious mind works all night and will help you fulfill this promise. Of course, if you're going to concentrate on nothing but noon and the smoke, you might as well forget the whole thing. Don't give in to yourself that easily; you are stronger than your addiction.

John L., an engineer and a former three-pack-a-day smoker, found the delay technique most valuable. He distracted his mind, concentrated on the task at hand, and found to his surprise that he had gone way beyond the noon deadline. Formerly, he would have smoked almost a pack of cigarettes between arising and 1:30 P.M.

4. After a meal, do not light up. Stand up from the table, if only for a few minutes. If for some reason you cannot leave the table, take a deep breath, hold it, and as you exhale, drop your jaw (you don't have to open your mouth) and let your shoulders droop. This will release tension and help break the pattern; nobody else needs to know what you're doing.

**REMEMBER:
NO UNCONSCIOUS, AUTOMATIC SMOKES
DELAY-DISTRACT — DISTRACT-DELAY
NO SMOKING AT THE END OF A MEAL**

More Basic Training — Correct Breathing

Further preparation for your first nonsmoking day includes deep diaphragmatic breathing, sometimes known as yoga breathing. This is an important part not only of your preparation, but later, of your heightened awareness techniques.

Diaphragmatic breathing is the natural, normal way of taking in oxygen. It's the way we were born to breathe, the way we breathe naturally during sleep. Somewhere along the line, children are taught to pull their shoulders back and take a breath in the chest, raising the shoulders. This only catches the diaphragm superficially and creates a very shallow breath.

The deep, full diaphragmatic breath — the singer's breath, the athlete's breath — does two things. First, it allows maximum expansion of the lungs, and thus, maximum oxygen intake. Second, it provides ten times the relaxation capability, energy, and endurance of the shallow breathing.

Use the diaphragmatic breathing technique often to release tension while you are cutting down on smoking. It's easy. Take a slow deep breath through your nose, putting the air into your abdomen. Think energy and hold. As you exhale slowly, like a balloon exhausting air, think, "discharging all my tension."

As you exhale SLOWLY through your lips, let your jaw drop and your shoulders droop. All the tension flows out of your body. In our tension-ridden times, this breathing exercise, done many times a day, will not only help prepare you for your *non*smoking life, but it will minimize your fatigue and improve your general health. You can practice diaphragmatic breathing any time and any place.

Advanced Maneuvers — Psychological Infiltration

You have already done a good job of cutting down on the smokes, and you have gone a long way toward breaking the reflex habit. Now to move on to some other valuable techniques — some brain work.

Before learning your heightened awareness techniques, you should establish "finger talking." This ideomotor activity is a fascinating phenomenon. Let's examine it.

Have you ever ridden in the passenger seat of a car, experienced a sudden thought or impression that the driver should apply his brakes, and pressed *your* foot down on the floorboard? Most of us have.

If you imagine and think of a time you experienced severe cold, your body could shudder. Conversely, if you imagine and think of the warm sun beating down upon you, you could feel warm.

A mother thinks her baby should open its mouth and opens her own.

Have you ever listened to a stutterer and noticed how your lips and tongue form the words he is trying to say?

The thought of something pleasurable produces a smile.

THE IDEA COMES FIRST, THEN THE MOTOR RESPONSE.

You can set your own response pattern — your signals to indicate or represent ideas from your subconscious mind.

Close your eyes and think, "Yes, yes, yes." Raise the finger that you would like to represent this answer. Then think, "No, no, no," and raise another finger, whichever you choose, to represent that answer. Keep the signals on the same hand. Make the fingers lift comfortably and easily. Their movements will become your private signals for conditioning. Keep the same signals for the same idea or answer. These finger signals can be used in many instances to obtain subconscious approval.

When you recall a pleasurable experience, you are contacting your subconscious, since you cannot at the same time be thinking of your business, your family, what you have to do, or whom you have to phone. At that moment your conscious mind is not operating. You have bypassed your critical thinking and are in an altered state of consciousness. It's that simple.

The same thing happens when you're so absorbed in a book you fail to hear someone call you. In both cases the conscious mind is set aside. This mental concentration in another area, away from the traffic of conscious thinking, is all that it takes to put you in an altered state of consciousness, which is nothing more than relaxing and allowing your subconscious mind to come forward.

You may ask your subconscious for affirmation in this way: *Is my subconscious mind willing to let me know that I can maintain my nonsmoking existence?* Let your "yes" finger lift. Although you are aware of the movement, the answer is coming from the subconscious mind; your conscious mind is not in operation.

Don't poke your finger up like a pencil. Rather, make a quick, short motion like an involuntary twitch. Some people expect the finger to lift without their help, which is impossible. You know the finger is lifting, but it is doing so automatically. You will understand finger signals better and derive a great deal of support from their use after you have learned the heightened awareness techniques.

When you have conquered your smoking addiction, you can continue using your finger signals in a way that can be very comforting — as an affirmation or form of approval from your inner self.

Here is an example from my own experience. I was scheduled to give a lecture on heightened awareness in a small town some two hours out of San Francisco, where I live. Everything went wrong. The person who was to pick me up by car had a mishap with the automobile, and at the last minute, I had to catch a bus.

By the time I arrived at the town, I was already an hour late. The only way to reach the lecture hall was by taxi. I had to phone for one and endure yet another half-hour delay. Being punctual by nature, I was extremely annoyed. The people expecting to hear me were strangers. I felt ruffled and nervous.

Finally, standing at the door of the hall, I took a deep breath. Quickly, I recalled a sunset scene I love and relaxed on exhalation. Then I asked my question, "Is my subconscious mind willing to let me know that I can give one of the best talks of my career?" I let my "yes" finger lift. This took less than a minute, and immediately, a feeling of relaxation and calm spread through me. I felt a tremendous boost of confidence and self-affirmation. My mental attitude was "set" to give a successful performance, and that was exactly what happened.

Given these same circumstances, I might well have succumbed to anxiety and allowed the pressure to ruin my presentation. Remember, however, that *pressure is not something anyone does to you. Pressure is your own response to outside stimuli.* You can learn to handle pressure in the new way. The more pressure there is around you, the more you relax. Use your diaphragmatic breathing, exhaling slowly, dropping the jaw and drooping the shoulders.

You cannot be uptight and relaxed at the same time.

The more hectic the situation, the more relaxed you should be. If you do this, you will find that you have changed your inner rhythm from tense to relaxed, and you will be able to handle outside pressure with inner calm and objective thinking. Add this to your finger approval and you have got it made!

Conditioned finger talking can become a powerful aid to you in times of anxiety and doubt. It can boost your confidence, allowing for a calm, productive approach. If practiced daily, this "yes" finger signal can change failure to success, pessimism to optimism, and become a secret aid in facing any stressful situation. So, if you find yourself tense when everyone around you is smoking, or under pressure from a frustrating circumstance, use your finger signal to confirm your nonsmoking existence.

Some smokers who have been told to quit by their doctors consciously believe they want to quit and seem anxious to quit; yet, when asked for subconscious approval, they signal with their "no" finger.

Unfortunately, these people, for various reasons, may subconsciously feel they deserve self-punishment. In such cases, further therapy may be needed to eliminate self-destructive ideas and their need to punish themselves. Once they have solved their guilt feelings, these people have no trouble lifting their "yes" finger for nonsmoking approval.

More on the Subconscious — Your Greatest Ally

Have you ever had a bad dream or nightmare and felt your body jerk? It happens all the time. Why does your body respond? It's only a dream. The scientific explanation is that your subconscious mind and nervous system have no way of differentiating between imagination and reality. *Everything* that goes on in your brain is reality to the subconscious mind and nervous system.

You have heard the words *conscious* and *subconscious* applied to the brain. The subconscious mind is not something separate. The brain is one, made up of different parts. The conscious mind is what you recognize as the doer, the thinker.

Everyone has had the experience of awakening minutes before the alarm rings. The subconscious mind at work. Or, you may go to sleep with an unsolved problem and awaken in the morning with a solution. Again, your subconscious mind in action. The subconscious mind is the intuitive, creative part of the mind; like an obedient child, it takes orders literally and carries them out.

The subconscious mind also handles all your involuntary body functions even when you are asleep, under anesthesia, or knocked unconscious. It protects you and wants the best for you. All you have to do is let go of conscious thinking, feed your subconscious mind constructive thoughts tied up with the image of the NEW YOU, and repeat this conditioning. Conditioning means training — repeatedly telling yourself in relaxation how you expect to think and what you expect to do.

Your subconscious mind follows your conscious instructions and thoughts, both positive and negative. You can make it your greatest ally by feeding it constructive, healthy information, thereby reprogramming negative, destructive blueprints. By this reprogramming, you can impress your subconscious mind with anything you want to accomplish or become.

The nature of the subconscious mind is to protect the organism for survival, health, and well-being. Why clobber your subconscious mind with faulty notions when you can feed it health-promoting ones? You have a choice.

One psychiatrist said, "It's the surly bird that catches the germ." Negative thinking saps the energy and accomplishes nothing, while positive, pleasant thoughts generate health and well-being. You can command, demand, and decree exactly the type of thinking you will do — most of the time.

"Aha," some may say, "this sounds like the positive thinking game."

No, it is not. The thinking is positive, but it is not mere positive thinking. For instance, suppose a man lacked confidence and, in an effort to change, from morning until night he tried thinking positively, saying to himself, "I am confident. I am confident. I am confident." This would *not* help him if deep within, he continued to feel inadequate. Why should he listen to an inadequate person?

Yet, by setting his conscious mind aside, using the heightened awareness techniques, and creating in his subconscious a new, confident image, this same man could realize his innate potential.

The conscious mind often says thumbs down, you can't do it. The subconscious mind knows better.

Another Caution: Don't Think Ahead

Anxiety is created by thinking ahead. If you think, "I wonder if I'm going to make it?" you've already said no. I-wonder-if projects the present into the unknown future. Never permit I-wonder-if to take hold. If you catch yourself with this negative thought, instantly replace it with a positive, constructive one.

Think of your life in general, and this work in particular, as ONE DAY, HERE AND NOW. THAT'S ALL THERE IS. If you plan today, schedule today, and act today to the best of your ability, the future will take care of itself. As Alan Watts commented, "For those who do not live fully in the present, the future is a hoax."

Live your nonsmoking program ONE DAY AT A TIME by practicing heightened awareness exercises each day to help reinforce and maintain your goal.

There are some who prepare for the cutoff with great enthusiasm and make a game of it. T.W., a pressured businessman and two-pack-a-day smoker, was such an individual. He told me that he enjoyed shouting out to whoever would listen, "Now I'm lighting a cigarette and I'm going to smoke it." Strangers in restaurants who witnessed his strange behavior might have thought him odd, but this only amused him. He also hung a daily chart on his bathroom wall listing any automatic, unconsciously lit cigarettes. There were none. As he intensified his awareness of each smoke, he cut down to two cigarettes a day — one week ahead of his scheduled cutoff date. When he telephoned to report his success, I advised him to move forward immediately to self-exploration and the reason for his first cigarette. At the end of that session, I advised him to smoke his last cigarette, confirming as he put it out, *"This is it. This is the last cigarette I am smoking."*

Then immediately, he was to go forward to conditioning, using the heightened awareness techniques. Should you find yourself in the same situation, you can follow the same procedure and move to chapter nine.

Chapter 9

Mental Tricks
Or, How to Reshuffle
Your Thinking

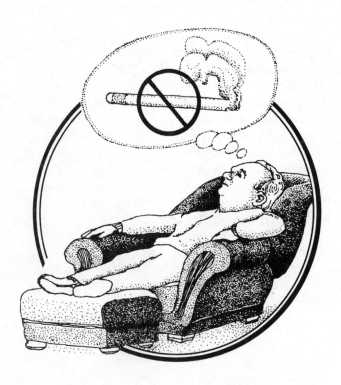

(Games people can play)

> I wake to sleep, and take my waking slow . . .
> I learn by going where I have to go.
> THEODORE ROETHKE

Training in Heightened Awareness

Five main elements form the foundation for the heightened awareness process. Later, you will build on this foundation with specific directions.

1. BODY RELAXATION. Deep relaxation of the body is essential. Deep relaxation might be called a form of hibernation. It's the type of relaxation Houdini achieved when he locked himself in a trunk under water. It's the type of relaxation animals demonstrate in times of danger when they simulate "dead" by quieting all body processes.

You can master similar body relaxation by repeated practice. The relaxation is progressive, starting slowly and moving rapidly as you continue. The process takes varying lengths of time, depending on your state of relaxation when you start. If you are tense, it will take longer than if you are relaxed when you begin.

However, with repeated rehearsal, even the most tense person can learn how to achieve the relaxed state quickly. Only you can relax your body. It's a do-it-yourself process that improves steadily as you practice, until finally, you achieve the relaxation almost instantly on the signal of your self-hypnosis conditioning.

2. IMAGINATION. Your imagination is much more powerful than your will power. Emil Coue said, "When the will and

the imagination are in conflict, the imagination gains the day." The Chinese said it another way, "One picture is worth a thousand words." Your imagination is a power.

Test your imagination. Close your eyes and imagine you are sinking your teeth into a sour, juicy lemon. Hold that image and soon you will start to salivate. If you told yourself on command to salivate immediately, you would find it difficult.

3. CONCENTRATION. Concentration is important to your exercise. Holding your attention on your exercise will hold the brain in the "altered state" to *help you toward your nonsmoking goal*. The self-hypnosis relaxation becomes a state of passive receptivity that shuts out the exterior world and slows down the stream of conscious thoughts so that you can zero in to a concentration on a deeper, intuitive level of awareness.

Test your concentration. Hold a pencil between two fingers of an outstretched hand. Concentrate with all your mental power on the tip of the pencil. As you concentrate, keep mumbling aloud rapidly, "I can drop it. I can drop it. I can drop it." You will find that if you are really concentrating, you *cannot* and will not drop it. The reason for this is, in order to drop the pencil, you would have to break your concentration on the tip and give your brain a different order — to separate your fingers. As long as you really concentrate on the tip, you can mumble, "I can drop it, I can throw it," or anything you want, and you will not let go of the pencil.

The story of Nurmi, the Flying Finn, illustrates the importance of concentration. Nurmi, an old-time Finnish runner, was a champion who had been winning every race, but on one occasion he lost. When his furious manager asked him what happened, Nurmi was said to reply, "In the middle of the race I thought of my check."

Your complete concentration is vital. If in the beginning your mind wanders, pull it back again and concentrate on the weights on your upper eyelids. This mental activity will help you increase your concentration in other areas of your life.

4. REPETITION. Hitler said that if you repeat a lie often enough, you soon get to believe it. The same holds for the truth. The word is power and has been used as a therapeutic approach. The brain works on electrical impulses. Repeated programming of the right, constructive word deeply impresses it on the mind. Like a phonograph record, the more it is played, the deeper the grooves. Therefore, by repeatedly introducing the thought, *I'm a permanent nonsmoker. I no longer need that crutch. And this time I will make it stick!*, you intensify its meaning in your brain. Experiencing the new thought over and over again will finally give it power and endurance.

Psychological researchers in the Soviet Union have demonstrated the reaction to words with electroencephalograms. Threatening words like *fear, death,* and *pain* showed up as excitation on the graph, while words like *calm, beauty, harmony,* and *tranquility* produced a quiet, at-ease tracing. The right word, the soothing word, reacts on the nervous system in a salutary way.[4]

5. EXPECTANCY. With these techniques, *expectancy* does not connote *command* or *demand*. Expectancy, in this case, is a kind of belief or conviction. It is an inner knowing that you are moving in a new direction. By practicing deep relaxation techniques, you can convince yourself to believe what you tell yourself.

The body is the instrument you're learning to play, and, like any other learning, the more you practice, the better you get. The daily conditioning of your mind with heightened awareness relaxation will become a constructive discipline, giving you a new centering of your vital forces. The word *discipline* is often associated with punishment. The dictionary defines it as coming from disciple, meaning learner. All discipline is self-serving.

Reviewing the above, you can readily see that the heightened awareness practice is self-motivated. No one else can relax your body, concentrate for you, or feel and hold your sense of expectancy. The guru you are working with is your own brain. *You are the guru.* Only you can push that button in your head. Only you can become a permanent nonsmoker!

Chapter 10

Heightened Awareness
Or, Self-Hypnosis

(Think back to the beginning)

> I have learned this at least by my experiment:
> that if one advances confidently in the
> direction of his dreams, and endeavors to
> live the life which he has imagined, he will
> meet with success in common hours.
> HENRY DAVID THOREAU

Heightened awareness or, as some people call it, self-hypnosis, is a process of relaxing the body and releasing tension and stress from the mind. By turning off conscious thinking, new and desirable patterns of thought and behavior are introduced. You might call it goal-directed meditation, the difference being that in meditation, you allow random thoughts to enter and depart without censorship, while in self-hypnosis, you focus on a specific change or improvement in your life, sticking with one problem — in this case the smoking problem — until it is resolved. An added bonus to this practice is the experience of deep, progressive relaxation, which encourages feelings of tranquility, harmony, and inner balance.

Scientists have not been able to prove exactly what happens in the brain during heightened awareness or hypnosis. The results, however, have been clearly demonstrated. Electroencephalogram (EEG) studies prove that during heightened awareness, brain waves are not in a sleeping, but a waking, state. The knee-jerk and galvanic-skin tests conclusively demonstrate that the person is not asleep or unconscious, but rather in a state of heightened mental awareness. Memory feats, athletic prowess, positive emotional changes, and even physical structural body changes have been documented.

In the same way, most surprisingly, many heavy smokers have reported that with their heightened awareness conditioning, they have lost all desire to smoke within a day or two, or for some, immediately.

The heightened awareness techniques are tools you can use to quickly motivate yourself to do many things, particularly quitting smoking. What you tell yourself during heightened awareness, you will definitely carry out.

There is a faulty notion that heightened awareness (or hypnosis) weakens the mind. Sometimes when people see a subject slip quickly into the relaxed state on a given signal, they fail to understand that this person has practiced and conditioned *himself* to do this. Contrary to weakening his mind, he has strengthened it to achieve greater concentration and performance.

A hypnotized person can accept or reject any suggestion. His subconscious mind protects him at all times. If he chooses to speak during heightened awareness, he can and will say only what he wants to say for his best interest.

Actually, the subject can lie beautifully if it's to his advantage. His face wears a relaxed, masklike expression with no telltale lines. But, since he conditions himself only with salutary, constructive ideas in self-hypnosis, he would certainly want to accept them.

People ask, "If I put myself into a state of relaxation through self-hypnosis, how do I come out?" Easily. You put yourself into the state and you bring yourself out simply by thinking that you're coming out. This can be done by counting from one to three and by opening your eyes on three. Or, if necessary, you can tell yourself, "I'll open my eyes and come up wide awake and alert" any time you decide. At all times you are doing and thinking the entire process and *you are always in control*.

Naturally, common sense indicates that you will not put yourself into a state of self-hypnosis when you should be consciously alert and awake. These principles should never be practiced at the wheel of a car, in an elevator, or in any place where you want to be fully, consciously aware of what you are doing and where you are. While cerebral activity is enhanced during heightened awareness relaxation, motor reactions may be slightly decreased. The wise thing, therefore, is to do the relaxation exercise in a comfortable, safe place; when you finish, take a deep diaphragmatic breath and come up wide awake and alert.

Some Do's and Don'ts in Practice

Frequently, the feeling of heightened awareness is so relaxing and comfortable that a person is loath to come out of it. Remaining in this state for a lengthy stay, while pleasant indeed, is not conditioning. In fact, short repetitions of this exercise are more beneficial for making changes. If the session is too long, the mind is likely to wander away from the main issue. There is also the danger of falling asleep.

Sleep is beneficial when you need it, but if you are sleeping, you are not working on change. Another danger of frequently falling asleep while practicing is that you may condition yourself to fall asleep *every time* you do the exercise, and accomplish nothing. Therefore, insist on coming up when the exercise ends. That is, when you have completed that session's work on conditioning and reinforcing, force yourself to come up.

Do not expect too much of yourself in the beginning. The ability to relax grows with practice. Also, *do not analyze* during practice. Do not ask yourself, "How am I doing? I wonder if I'm doing it?" When you let such thoughts enter your mind, you definitely are *not* doing it. In fact, such thoughts break the concentration and interfere with your progressive relaxation. People who analyze are doing two things: trying to concentrate on inner feelings and thinking of something else. The *two are incompatible*. In heightened awareness, you are shutting out external stimuli so that you can utilize and work with your own inner experience of mind and body.

At first you may feel that nothing is happening. Never mind; keep practicing daily. The rewards will gratify and surprise you. Remember, you cannot expect immediate perfection in heightened awareness any more than you can expect instant perfection playing the piano. The body is the instrument; the more you practice, the better you become. Your willingness, your receptivity, and your continued daily conditioning will bring the best results. Don't push. Don't press. Simply concentrate on your body relaxation and the imagery. Let go and let it happen.

Norman L., an aggressive businessman, could not tolerate anyone telling him what or how to do anything. After learning his self-hypnosis training instructions to quit smoking, he decided to do his own reprogramming, using his own suggestion and verbalization. Every time he thought of a cigarette during his heightened awareness practice, he told himself, "I will not smoke. I will never again smoke another cigarette."

Here, he pitted determination against desire (the I-try-hard-syndrome), exactly contrary to the principles of this work, and got the I-try-hard results. Within a short time he returned to his full smoking schedule.

REMEMBER. NEVER THINK OR SAY I WILL NOT SMOKE!

If you must use your own wording, be sure it is semantically appropriate. Be affirmative: "I am a permanent nonsmoker. I no longer need that crutch."

You've been smoking for years, and you've been behaving and thinking along fixed patterns. Now you want to change your patterns, but the old ones are stronger than the new. You must be willing to work — to practice your heightened awareness techniques, to re-educate your mind, and to retrain your reflexes and your thinking. Habits die hard. It takes reinforcement, several times a day to imprint the new patterns on your subconscious mind until they are ultimately your own. It's like driving a car with an unfamiliar gear shift. At first, you may have to think about shifting, but soon it becomes your new automatic response. The advantage of this technique is that it allows you to make the changes quickly, easily, and more comfortably.

The heightened awareness techniques are *not* cures for all ills. They are not intended to replace psychological, psychiatric, or medical assistance. The techniques are given here for only one reason — to help you quit smoking permanently and to give you a tool for releasing tension while doing so.

The Day You Quit: Back to Your First Smoke

Sit down in a quiet place. Create an atmosphere of harmony and tranquility, a relaxation of mind and body. Close your eyes and, just like in a daydream or reverie, take yourself back in time to that very first cigarette or smoke you ever had.

See yourself taking that smoke and analyze why you did it. To show off? To be part of an "in" group? To feel grown up? Did you do it on a dare? Or, was it a revolt? Perhaps you identified with someone.

When you know the reason, tell yourself, "I am no longer that person. That reason for smoking is no longer valid. At this time in my life, I don't have to behave that way."

Smoking is not a symbol of fellowship; it is not proof of maturity or confidence; it is not a symbol of bravery or independence. The smoke has nothing whatsoever to do with these things. After years of smoking, you have conditioned yourself with these notions associated with smoking, an association that is invalid.

Use your finger talk. Call on your trusted ally, your subconscious mind. Ask yourself this question, "Is my subconscious mind willing to have me disconnect from those childish reasons for smoking?" Let your "yes" finger lift. Let your subconscious mind affirm your willingness. Let your subconscious mind run the show.

If, during your deep relaxation, your mind cannot recall your first smoke, don't be discouraged. It is not essential, only helpful for you to know and disconnect from the reason that led you to take that first smoke. You can proceed by asking yourself, "Whatever the reason for my first smoke, whenever it happened, is my subconscious mind willing for me to disconnect from that reason?" Let your "yes" finger lift. The results will be equally effective.

Whether or not you know the reason for your first smoke, you have disconnected from that early time and are now ready for your last smoke.

The age at which a person first smoked and his reasons for beginning to smoke are very revealing. Some had their first cigarette as early as six. Others began out of Oedipal motivations.

Women took their first cigarette because "Dad smoked," and they wanted to emulate him. Men identified with the mother and smoked "because my mother smoked."

An amazing story came from a forty-year-old stockbroker who said he smoked his first cigarette when he was four. When I asked if other kids were around, he said, "My brother." "How old was your brother?" I asked. "Two," he answered. "Why did you do it?" was the next question. "Because my mother scolded us about touching matches."

Can you picture the scene? Two babies lighting matches and puffing cigarettes!

L.T., a three-pack-a-day smoker, went back to the age of nine, when her grandmother caught her stealing a cigarette. The grandmother, herself a heavy smoker, said, "I never want you to steal cigarettes. From now on, you will smoke in front of me." Three cigarettes were doled out to the girl daily; on her sixteenth birthday, the grandmother tied a whole pack of cigarettes on her birthday gift.

Later, the woman laughed at her naive grandmother, because she said she had already been smoking a pack a day for several years.

Your Last Smoke

Before starting to practice your self-hypnosis relaxation techniques, have the last smoke. Make an occasion of it. As you put out that last smoke, make a firm commitment in your mind. Tell yourself, *"This is it. This is my last smoke."*

Chapter 11

Get Ready,
Get Set

Or, Go

(Forward, please)

"Don't just do something," Buddha
said, "stand there!"

Your Heightened Awareness or Self-Hypnosis Formula

The heightened awareness formula is first outlined, then followed by the actual wording. Memorize the wording and dictate it onto a tape, or, if you prefer, have someone else dictate it for you.

When practicing the formula, consider yourself both operator and subject. While one part of your mind is giving instructions, the other part is following them. This exercise should take four to five minutes, no more, and should be practiced SLOWLY, as if you had all day.

1. INDUCTION. Eye fixation on a spot without blinking, deep diaphragmatic breath. Hold the position. Think *prana* (your conditioning signal) as you simultaneously close your eyes, drop your jaw, and exhale very slowly, like a balloon exhausting air.

2. YOUR PEACEFUL SCENE. Choose a relaxing, peaceful scene and stay with the same scene at all times. Review the scene, using one sense at a time: seeing, naming the things you see, hearing, smelling.

3. EYELOCK. Let your upper eyelids get more and more relaxed to a point where they do not want to open. Then imagine you have weights on the upper eyelids, making them feel *heavy and locked, heavy and locked.*

4. USE YOUR IMAGINATION. Imagine you are looking at four numbers written by a skywriter: 100, 99, 98, and 97. Count the numbers in your mind. Each time you count a number, see it fade into the sky. Let your jaw go looser and lower. Even if it seems impossible to go looser, think of it as looser.

5. SUGGESTION. Repeat three times: I'm a permanent nonsmoker. I no longer need that crutch. And this time I make it stick. (Use the last phrase even if you've never quit before.)

6. ADD THREE AFFIRMATIONS. I want this to happen. I *expect* this to happen. I *allow* and *deserve* to have this happen. Stress the words *allow* and *deserve*.

7. SUBCONSCIOUS APPROVAL AT EACH PRACTICE. "Is my subconscious mind willing to let me know that I can maintain my nonsmoking and that I'm not bothered by others smoking around me?" Let your "yes" finger lift.

8. PICTURE YOUR NEW SELF-IMAGE. Someone offers you a smoke, your former brand, at the end of a meal and you say, *"No, thank you. I've quit smoking permanently."*

9. THINK AT EACH PRACTICE, "NEXT TIME I'LL GO DEEPER." You will if you practice daily.

10. COUNT FROM THREE TO ONE AND OPEN YOUR EYES ON ONE. Three, I'm coming up; two, I'm more and more alert; and one, I'm wide awake and alert.

"How long do I stick with my nonsmoking suggestion?" is a common question asked by people working with self-hypnosis. The time varies for each individual. With strong motivation, changes happen quickly, sometimes instantly. Other times, when there is subconscious resistance, repeated conditioning is necessary to make the nonsmoking suggestion stick.

"How will I know?" is another frequent question. As you continue your self-hypnosis practice daily, the subconscious mind will give you a clear signal. A philosopher once said, *"Learning is not knowledge until you've heard it in your head."*

For example, T.L., a real estate broker, reported that after practicing for two months, he awakened during the night, thinking, "I'm a permanent nonsmoker. I no longer need that crutch."

H.B., a young legal secretary, reported that after practicing three months, every time she came to her nonsmoking suggestion, it seemed to float into her mind from an outside force.

Since the self-hypnosis or heightened awareness techniques are designed to release tension, you can use them later to relax whenever you need to.

Heightened Awareness or Self-Hypnosis Practice

The mind works at a tremendous speed, processing anywhere from 400 to 500 words a minute. A speaker can talk only at a rate of 125 to 150 words per minute.

It follows, then, that if you are practicing with a tape, you will need more time (about seven to ten minutes) than if you are running through the formula in your head. In the beginning, you can run through the mental practice, without vocalizing, in about five minutes. With repeated practice, you can finally do it in one minute or less.

The cassette tape, however, helps the beginner to establish the feeling of this special kind of relaxation. If you plan to use the tape, work with it for several weeks. Then rely on your memory, using the tape at intervals for reinforcement. Self-hypnosis is both an art and a science. Like any other skill, the more you do it, the better you become.

When you practice, think of yourself as both the operator and the subject. While one part of your mind gives instructions, another part of your mind follows. At first you may feel that nothing is happening. Never mind. Keep practicing daily. Very soon the discipline becomes a way of life. Finally, with daily conditioning, you can attain the capacity for instant, deep relaxation anytime you need it. Remember, your key word is *prana*. *Prana* is a word used in yoga, meaning "life force." Whenever the word *prana* comes to mind, take a deep breath and instantly associate it with deep relaxation.

THE GAME AT A GLANCE

1. You have broken your reflex patterns and have cut down smoking.
2. You have set your finger-talking signals.
3. You have explored the reason for taking your first smoke and have disconnected from that early association with smoking.
4. You have smoked your last cigarette, cigar, or pipe.
5. You are now starting your heightened awareness or self-hypnosis practice and plan to make it a daily ritual in your life.

All you have to do from now on is hang in there and remember, the first smoke is the criminal and you will definitely resist taking it.

A tip of the hat to you! You are on the road to better health and happiness.

YOUR PRACTICE BEGINS

INSTRUCTIONS

You begin. Make the body comfortable. Close out everything from the outside world. Concentrate. Fix your eyes on a spot in a wide-open stare without blinking.

The vision may blur or become hazy. This is normal, since the eyes are the smallest muscles in the body and tire the quickest. As you think your key word *prana*, DRAG THE WORD OUT in your mind. Simultane-

VERBALIZATION

(Mental, not spoken) *My body is relaxed and comfortable as I focus my eyes on a spot in a wide-open stare. As I stare at that spot, the new image of myself comes before me: a permanent nonsmoker.*

Very quickly my eyes become tired; my lids, heavier, heavier, and heavier still. Now I roll my eyeballs back into my head* and take a deep breath in the diaphragm and HOLD. As I

---

*Do not roll eyeballs back if you're wearing contact lenses. Either remove your contacts or simply stare.

ously relax the eyes, drop the jaw, and exhale *slowly* like a balloon exhausting air.

think my key word prana, *my eyes relax; the jaw drops as I exhale SLOWLY like a balloon exhausting air.*

My tongue lies loose and quiet in the floor of my mouth, quieting all its words. I quiet all the thoughts in my head and take my mind to a peaceful scene in nature.

INSTRUCTIONS

Scene. This scene can go back to your childhood or it can be anywhere or anytime in your life when you felt completely relaxed and at peace. If you cannot think of such a scene, conjure one up in your mind, like a painting, a picture, or a scene that is relaxing and peaceful to you.

Always use the same peaceful scene. Should you later decide on a better scene, change it, but once established, keep the same scene for all of your practice.

If you've made up an imaginary scene, just imagine what you would see, hear, or smell. Conditioning yourself to the same scene becomes a signal that triggers relaxation.

INSTRUCTIONS

Scene

Sight

VERBALIZATION

The scene comes into my mind clearly, vividly, as if I am there. Now I will review the experience using one sense at a time. Taking sight, I look around and review all the colors and nuances of colors. I see them all again clearly, vividly as I go deeper and deeper into DEEP relaxation.

Hearing

My ears are tuned to the sounds around me. Sounds, movement, even silence. I can hear them, as I go deeper and deeper into DEEP relaxation.

Smell

My nostrils remember the smell of the air, fragrances, odors. The whole scene is in sharp clarity, as I go deeper and deeper into this marvelous feeling of DEEP, SOOTHING relaxation.

INSTRUCTIONS

VERBALIZATION

Eyelock

As I continue to stay in my scene, I bring my attention back to the eyelids and let my upper lids droop over my lower lids, looser, looser, and still looser. And then I imagine and pretend that my upper eyelids have weights on them, making my eyelids so heavy. They feel heavy and locked, heavy and locked, heavy and locked. And, while I'm pretending that lead is on them, even if I want to open them, they just don't feel like opening.

The words "heavy and locked," "heavy and locked," "heavy and locked" should be repeated rapidly in succession.

A blanket of serenity spreads over the entire body.

That same feeling of relaxation from the eyelids flows down my facial muscles. My jaw goes looser still as the feeling spreads through my body like a blanket of serenity. Completely relaxed. Completely relaxed.

INSTRUCTIONS

Use Your Imagination

Numbers in the Sky
You don't really have to see
them. But you can pretend and
imagine seeing them. As you
think of a number, think of letting your jaw go looser and
looser, even if it seems impossible to go looser. Silently hear
yourself singing the numbers in
your head.

Suggestion
Repeat *slowly* in your mind
three times, even if you haven't
quit before, "And this time I
make it stick."

VERBALIZATION

*I imagine looking up at the sky
at four numbers a skywriter has
written from 100 to 97. I will
count each number. Each time I
count a number, it fades into the
sky and I double my relaxation.*
100 *The number fades and my
jaw gets looser and looser.*
99 *The number disappears and
I make my relaxation
greater.*
98 *The number fades and I go
deeper and deeper into
relaxation.*
97 *All the numbers vanish and
I let myself drift and float,
drift and float.*
*Now, I'm ready for my
suggestion:*
I'm a permanent nonsmoker.
I no longer need that crutch.
And this time I make it stick.
I'm a permanent nonsmoker.
I no longer need that crutch.
And this time I make it stick.
I'm a permanent nonsmoker.
I no longer need that crutch.
And this time I make it stick.

INSTRUCTIONS

Three affirmations:
Stress the words *allow* and *deserve.* "Allow" means your
mind is open and receptive to
these thoughts. "Allow" means
you are willing to transcend old
patterns for new ones. "Deserve" means you value your
life and feel that you deserve
health and a longer, better life.

VERBALIZATION

Now my three affirmations:
I want this to happen.

I expect this to happen.
*I allow and deserve to have this
happen.*

Subconscious Approval

Is my subconscious mind willing to let me know that I can maintain my nonsmoking permanently and that I'm not bothered by others smoking around me? (My "yes" finger lifts.)

Image One
When you see yourself rejecting the smoke, take a deep breath and feel the pride in your achievement.

Now I see myself at the end of a meal with others. I'm very comfortable without a cigarette. And, as I watch others lighting up, I'm thinking the cigarette is not a symbol of friendship. The cigarette is not a relaxer. The cigarette is poison. Someone offers me a cigarette from a pack, the kind I used to smoke, and I say, "No thank you. I've quit smoking permanently." When they move away with the pack, I feel so proud of myself and take a deep breath.

INSTRUCTIONS

Image Two
One year from the time you quit smoking, imagine yourself at a gathering. See yourself rejecting the smoke again and take a deep breath of satisfaction.

VERBALIZATION

I'm at a party. It's been a whole year since I quit smoking. I never felt better, never looked better. It's been a remarkable year. Many people are smoking around me. And, as I watch them, I'm thinking how lucky I am to be rid of that killing habit. Someone comes over and offers me a smoke, the kind I used to use. I say, "No thank you, I quit smoking permanently a year ago." When they move away I feel so proud of my achievement and take a deep breath.

INSTRUCTIONS	VERBALIZATION
NEXT TIME I WILL GO DEEPER. This must be thought in each practice.	*Next time I will go deeper.*
Arousal Any time you wish to come up instantly, all you have to do is say so in your mind, that is, "I'll open my eyes and be instantly wide awake and alert." You are controlling the entire process from beginning to end.	*Now I will count from three to one and open my eyes on the count of one, very pleased that I can do self-hypnosis and confident that I can maintain my nonsmoking existence with an uplift of spirit that will stay with me. Three. Coming up. Feeling fine.* *Two. More and more alert. Feeling good.* *One. Wide awake, alert, feeling wonderful, and I take another deep breath and come up wide awake and alert.*

Suggestion before sleep: "I'm a permanent nonsmoker. I no longer need that crutch. And this time I make it stick." The subconscious mind works all night and will strengthen your thought during the nighttime hours of sleep. Go to sleep with the expectation that this new condition will happen.

Expectation: A prediction of things to come, a promise to yourself that must be sustained and maintained by your new input of thought, "I'm a permanent nonsmoker. I no longer need that crutch." Your mental reinforcement creates cause and effect. Thought energy is the cause; thought form is the effect.

Each morning: Before jumping out of bed, tell yourself, "Just for today, I am strongly motivated to control the smoke. Just for today." One day at a time. Not thinking about results, just doing it. The results will take care of themselves.

Congratulations! You are a permanent nonsmoker.

You've made a trade. You have given up smoking for a longer life. Doctors claim that the life span is increased many years when you quit smoking.

You have given up smoking for clean, healthy, pink lungs, so that oxygen can enter your lungs without obstruction of nicotine residue.

You have given up smoking for more energy, more stamina.

You have given up smoking for a clean-smelling mouth and fresh-smelling breath.

You have given up smoking for an upsurge of confidence. The realization that you have broken an addiction is a tremendous boost of confidence in your own being to do anything you wish.

Indeed! *You have made a trade — all in your favor.*

Chapter 12

The Take-over
Or, I Am the Guru

(Your first day of freedom)

> No man is free who is not
> master of himself.
> EPICTETUS

Congratulations! At last, you have decided not only to quit smoking permanently, but to work hard to make this decision a reality. As you move toward your first day of freedom from nicotine enslavement, change all small habits. Don't sit in the same spot for breakfast; choose a different place as a symbol of the new cycle in your life.

Don't sit where you formerly sat smoking, eating, or watching television. Change patterns at work. Do something different. Just moving your desk to a slightly new position or rearranging your desk-top material can be symbolic of your new lifestyle. Consider your first nonsmoking day as the beginning of a new life, a new road, a new way of living and thinking.

Your First Nonsmoking Day

Have a glass of water, adding a teaspoon of apple cider vinegar or the juice of half a lemon, and drink it as soon as you wake up, telling yourself, *"Just for today,* I am strongly motivated to control the smoke. *Just for today."*

Have breakfast and do your self-hypnosis exercise if at all possible. Visualize yourself at the end of this first day having successfully overcome the urge to smoke.

Many times during your first day, use your diaphragmatic breathing to release tension: hold, exhale *slowly* as you drop your jaw, drooping your shoulders. The slower you exhale the breath (like a balloon exhausting air through a tiny hole), the greater your relaxation. This will be very helpful but should not replace your heightened awareness practice.

After meals (for the first week), stand up immediately.

Work with the principles and techniques of heightened awareness one day at a time, not thinking of results. The results will take care of themselves. Say, "No thank you, I've quit smoking permanently," to anyone who offers you a smoke. Each time you verbalize the thought, you will feel an added confirmation of your goal.

Remind yourself that a thought for a smoke lasts only *seconds* in the brain; all you have to cope with is seconds. When the thought of a smoke enters your mind, pop something into your mouth, like gum or hard candy, or take a drink of water. And distract your mind. DISTRACT. DISTRACT. DISTRACT.

Tell yourself, *"The craving for the smoke won't kill me. The smoke will."*

Tell yourself, *"I'm not giving up pleasure. I'm giving up poison."*

Tell yourself, *"The first smoke is the criminal."*

Tell yourself, *"No matter what happens in my life, nothing and no one can make me take that first smoke."*

The positive suggestions you give to yourself are as effective, or even more effective, than those given to you by anyone else. Suggestions in self-hypnosis are deeply imprinted on the subconscious mind. They are like the sun shining through a window onto a piece of paper. The sun warms the paper, but if you direct it onto the paper through a one-inch tube, the concentrated heat will burn through. Similarly, the suggestions in self-hypnosis go deep within the brain, and the subconscious mind continues to strengthen the thoughts to bring them to reality.

Through your relaxation techniques, you will develop an instantaneous response to *your* given signals. As you continue developing this art, you will strengthen a built-in guidance system of the NEW YOU (the permanent nonsmoker), a system by which you will handle all of life's irritations and problems in a new way.

If you are frustrated, unhappy, or in the middle of a crisis, use your relaxation techniques to help you respond with a relaxed objectivity that does not require a smoke.

Philosopher William James said, "Any habit that isn't fed, is soon dead."

BELIEVE IT OR NOT,
VERY SOON, SOONER THAN YOU
THINK, ALL THOUGHTS OF SMOKING
WILL BE GONE FROM YOUR MIND AND
BODY.

Chapter 13

Controlling
The Insurgents
Or, The Ghosts of
the Three Stooges

(Just a flick of the finger)

> Great souls have wills; feeble
> ones have only wishes.
> CHINESE PROVERB

Your cells are loaded with nicotine. Even if you have practiced your relaxation exercise three to six times during that first day; even if you have told yourself, "I'm a permanent nonsmoker, I no longer need that crutch," your cells don't understand. They are confused and can't figure out what has happened. They have been addicted and accustomed to receiving the nicotine poison. They are pulling at you, crying for more, more, more poison.

You will help flush out some of the poison from your cells by drinking quantities of water during the first few nonsmoking days. Physical exercise, if you're accustomed to a workout, will help bring up a sweat and release some of the poison from your body. You can't fight the cells' craving directly, but don't give in. Do your relaxation exercise. Ride over the momentary craving by taking your mind to other thoughts and by popping something into your mouth. Relax. Distract. The cells will soon get the message and lose their craving. You'll be in charge.

"A smoker's craving seems to be more pronounced on arising in the morning when the blood pressure is low and the blood sugar is at a fasting level. Thus, the patient has a craving for a cigarette or two and possibly two or three cups of coffee or tea to get going."[5]

Some people experience a similar letdown in the late afternoon due to a drop in blood sugar. Cravings are accentuated; this time is usually coffee break for Americans and high tea for the English. Makes sense. But don't reach for a smoke. Pick up the blood sugar by taking a high-protein snack (protein chewables), orange juice, or both.

According to Blue, "Many of those trying to quit who have been heavy smokers for decades state that they have a depressed, weak, and nervous feeling, especially if they are exerting themselves. They claim that a cigarette relieves these symptoms. Nicotine, besides having a profound effect on the nervous system, also releases glycogen from the liver. This may explain why chewing gum or eating candy helps allay the craving for a cigarette."[6]

The ramifications of low blood sugar, or hypoglycemia, and its management have been a controversial medical subject for some time. Doctors state that, unless there is a carbohydrate imbalance, the blood sugar in the morning is normal. These doctors postulate that heavy smokers mask symptoms of hypoglycemia with the lift from the nicotine in cigarettes. Subsequently, the let-down, fatigue, and accompanying irritability (symptoms of hypoglycemia) become apparent only after they quit smoking: symptoms that are not so much from withdrawal of the smoke as they are from the hypoglycemia.

While various theories and investigations exist concerning this medical problem, it is not my intention to delve into them. Each individual should take stock of his physical condition and check with his doctor.

Regardless of any possible blood sugar imbalance, both doctors and nutritionists agree that a hearty breakfast provides needed energy to start the day. Heavy smokers who customarily depend on a lift from a cup of coffee and a smoke would do well to eat a nutritional breakfast to prevent the let-down.

Aside from the obvious medical factors (more and more doctors are employing the principles of self-hypnosis), your relaxation techniques and deep breathing exercises are particularly important for making the transition to your nonsmoking life.

Be creative! Depending upon your temperament, interests, and environment, come up with some custom-made devices for easing into your new, nonsmoking life. You might even want to share some of your more successful techniques with others.

It is advisable during the first week not to indulge in too much excitement or to put yourself into pressure-building situations. Instead, lie low, keep a low emotional profile, and relax as much as possible. By the end of the first week of their new nonsmoking lives, people report a renewal of *vitality*. All the senses are heightened to new awareness. Take smell. You had forgotten the marvelous smell of food, flowers, perfumes, trees, and the clean, fresh smell of a spring morning. And *confidence*. People who have broken the addiction also report feeling new enthusiasm and a confidence they have not experienced for a long time. An upsurge of energy and well-being inevitably accompanies the success in kicking the habit. Use these energies positively, channeling them into other interests, particularly physical exercise. Exercise and deep breathing allow more oxygen to enter the lungs, increasing circulation and revitalizing the lung tissues. Imagine the freedom from the shackles of addiction. Imagine the gratification of being able to walk out of your house without checking for your smoking paraphernalia. You are free!

Loneliness and boredom are threats to your new nonsmoking life. Become involved. Do something *fun* with your new energy. Don't stay at home and feel sorry for yourself. A movie, a weekend excursion, a romance . . . yes, even with your spouse! (A little extra energy goes a long way!)

Alcohol is another threat. With one too many drinks, the brain gets fuzzy and you can forget, losing control of awareness. You're back where you started if you light that first automatic smoke.

Each nonsmoking day becomes easier and easier. Just HANG IN THERE and remember, the first smoke brings back all the craving. Overcome the urge. Practice. Practice.

You will be free! You will have done something marvelous for *yourself*. Whatever happens, you know you won't have to have a smoke. This sense and *reality* of control spreads to all areas of your life. *You* are in charge.

Caution

Complacency and lack of self-hypnosis practice are your greatest dangers. Take the case of J.L., a forty-year-old man with two pressure-pumping businesses going at once. Even with the emotional powder keg of his work, he had quit smoking and maintained it remarkably well for one month. He felt extremely proud of his achievement, and rightfully so. But one week after he had quit, he discontinued his daily practice, feeling that he had it made.

The harmony of his home crashed when an old girlfriend arrived from out of town and asked to stay with him and his live-in girlfriend. They agreed, halfheartedly.

During her stay, the friend persisted in being overly affectionate to J.L., and the tension in the air mounted. Finally, one evening when the guest and J.L. were in a tight clinch, his live-in girlfriend exploded. In firm, straightforward language, she ordered the other woman to leave.

Hating confrontation, J.L. stormed out and headed for the first store for a pack of cigarettes. Yes, he was upset! And the old association of cigarette-relaxer grabbed him spontaneously.

Had he been willing to give several minutes daily to reminding himself of his nonsmoking life, he would not have succumbed to the first puff. Instead, he could have released his tension in a different way. But at the moment of stress, J.L. did nothing. He gave in to the old ghost of reflex habit, which allowed the two stooges, physiological need and psychological need, an opening to move in. Before long, he returned to full-schedule puffing. Naturally, the former pattern, twenty-five years old, was much stronger than the new thought — only one month old.

Emotional stress and pressure are difficult to eliminate. Most people live with them in one form or another. In many cases, they are actually the impetus for great accomplishments in art, literature, music, and science exploration *when you are in control and when you constructively channel them.*

Your heightened awareness techniques can help you survive such bad moments by reminding you that they are temporary.

Your practice will pay off, not only in maintaining your non-smoking existence, but in gaining the satisfaction of handling problems in a new way, by relaxation and creativity.

The first time you use relaxation techniques under pressure, you will experience an elation, a gratification, and a feeling of a new inner power. YOU ARE YOUR OWN GURU!

Chapter 14

The Pretender
Or, When the Guru
Isn't You

(Working on conflicts)

> A failure establishes only this,
> that our determination to succeed
> was not strong enough.
> BOVEE

In my twelve years of helping people to become permanent non-smokers using these heightened awareness techniques, I have had a record of 95 percent success — people who quit permanently. The 5 percent who did not failed for a variety of reasons.

Quitting to please someone else instills resentment and usually backfires. Subconsciously, the smoker may wish to punish the controlling individual or perhaps punish himself for unresolved guilt feelings. Such dynamics throw him back into smoking.

Sadly, I must admit that occasionally, after an excellent session in heightened awareness training, when it appears that their reasons for quitting have been accepted subconsciously, a few leave the session and immediately buy a pack of cigarettes.

This always baffles me. When I follow up and ask, "Why did you do that?" the answer is, "It won't work for me." *That's right!* If they have convinced themselves that it won't work, they have created a mental "set," and it *does not* and *will not* work. Perhaps they come to the training already convinced of this and just want to prove that it won't work. It may be the old story of the self against the self.

Faith or belief with a firm conviction creates cause and effect. What you believe to be true for you (good or bad), you will live to realize. It pays to watch your thinking. Negative thinking saps your energy and accomplishes nothing. You can choose which thoughts to dwell on and which to throw out. When negative thoughts occur, instantly take your mind to pleasant, constructive thoughts. Two thoughts cannot stay in the brain at the same time. Of course, every human being has mood swings now and then. But most of the time you can train yourself to focus on the cheerful side of thinking — most of the time. As Job said in the Bible, "The thing which I greatly feared is come upon me." (Job 3:25.)

Verbal programming, coupled with a desired image, sets the nervous system into automatic motion, and the subconscious goes to work to bring it to reality. The case of Margaret T., a forty-five-year-old teacher, illustrates this point. She had many misconceptions of self-hypnosis gained from stage hypnotists who gave the impression that they had power over people, a repulsive thought to this woman. Later, she confessed that before coming for her training, she was certain that it would not work for her. She kept telling herself after the training, "It will not work. It will not work," and of course it did not. She might have been kinder to herself and to her subconscious mind if she had changed the negative thought to, "It *can* work for me," or at least, "It might work for me," thus giving herself permission to explore a new path of thinking.

Then again, there are others, even years after having quit smoking, who now and then, under excitement, emotion, and pressure, have a flicker of the old craving. It's only a flicker and can easily be surmounted if they distract their minds and ride over the momentary feeling. Many do. Others give in, take that first cigarette, and become smokers again.

People with low frustration thresholds, people with what I call the immature I-want syndrome, find an excuse, at the least provocation, that throws them back into smoking. You might say that people of this makeup are spoiled, unaccustomed to being strict with themselves on any issue, and accustomed to having their way. They use the cigarette as a reward symbol.

Still, others with deep emotional problems may need professional help in working out their conflicts. But even they can quit smoking when these conflicts are resolved.

The Reward

You have squandered money on poison — the smokes. Figure your smoking expense for one year. Allot the same amount for some joy. Buy something, not something that you particularly need, but something you want and felt you could not afford. Be extravagant with that money! Do something lavish. *You deserve it!*

In my beginning is my end.
T. S. ELIOT

The end of this book is the same as the beginning.
Now you can say

I HAVE ONLY ONE LIFE AND ONE BODY.
I NEED MY BODY TO LIVE.
SMOKING IS POISON TO MY BODY.

(Pause)

I WAS NOT BORN SMOKING;
I CHOSE TO SMOKE.
NOW I CHOOSE *NOT* TO SMOKE.

Footnotes

[1]Ochsner, Alton, "The Health Menace of Tobacco," *American Scientist,* vol. 59, March-April 1971.

[2]Blue, J.A., "Cigarette asthma and tobacco allergy," *Annals of Allergy,* March 1970.

[3]*New England Journal of Medicine,* June 1, 1972.

[4]Platinov, I., "The Word, A Therapeutic Approach," (translated from the Russian).

[5]Blue, J.A., *Annals of Allergy,* March 1970.

[6]Ibid.

BEST SELLERS

SUCCESS THROUGH MIND POWER
How To Be A Winner In The Game Of Life
Roy Hunter, M.H.
Why is change so elusive? Because we are often told what to change but never taught how. Now there is a step-by-step course in how to make the changes you desire through Mind Power Exercise, a simple and systematic approach to positive action that can help ensure success in every aspect of life.
Paperback • $5.95 • 130 pages

FINANCIAL SUCCESS THROUGH CREATIVE MIND POWER
Originally Titled The Science of Getting Rich
Wallace D. Wattles
This small book is a practical manual intended for men and women whose most pressing need is for money; who wish to get rich first and philosophize after. It has been responsible for the successes of thousands of Mind Power students in the half-century since it was first published.
Paperback • $5.95 • 92 pages

MIRACLES ON DEMAND
The Short-Term Radical Hypnotherapy of Gil Boyne
Charles Tebbetts, Certified Hypnotherapist
Gil Boyne has been called the genius of short term, result-oriented therapy, and his unique methods are documented here in detailed case histories. This is a complete training course in hypnotism, from the pre-induction interview through suggestibility tests, induction techniques, trance deepening methods, testing in trance and back-to-awareness procedures. Also includes an explanation of five major schools of psychology and how best to use them with hypnotherapy.
Hardcover • $37.50 • 521 pages

UNLOCK YOUR MIND AND BE FREE WITH HYPNOTHERAPY
Edgar A. Barnett, M.D.
Written by a medical doctor who now practices exclusively as a hypnotherapist, this dramatic book presents fascinating case studies in which hypnosis is the demonstrated key to solving emotional difficulties. Includes sections on self-hypnosis and self-analysis, and age regressions.
Paperback • $8.95 • 155 pages

TOTAL MIND POWER
Donald L. Wilson, M.D., Certified Hypnotherapist
How you can unlock the secrets to better health and happiness. Dr. Wilson's best-selling book teaches you easily learned, powerful techniques for tapping the other 90% of your mind.
Hardcover • Illustrated • 254 pages • $9.95

THE MIRACLE OF MIND POWER
Dan Custer
Enjoy better health, greater happiness and increased prosperity through the dynamic power of your mind. This stimulating and inspiring book is full of methods for tapping that power which you can start putting to work immediately.
Paperback • 263 pages • $7.95

HYPNOTHERAPY
Dave Elman
In this major work Eman creates a forceful and dynamic presentation of hypnosis as a lightning-fast and amazingly effective tool in a wide range of therapies. A summation of Elman's theories and techniques, it is a classic in the literature on hypnotism.
Hardcover • 336 pages • $24.00

HYPNOTISM & MEDITATION
Ormond McGill, Certified Hypnotherapist
An operational manual for Hypnomeditation. Every process is clearly explained and detailed formulas are given. Fifteen days with Hypnomeditation will change your life!
Paperback • 99 pages • $5.95

HYPNOSIS AND POWER LEARNING
Pierre Clement, Hypnotherapist
A do-it-yourself tool for self-hypnosis, divided into three parts: 1) Getting acquainted with hypnosis; 2) Acquiring self-hypnosis; 3) Utilizing self-hypnosis as a powerful learning method, including strengthening of will power, concentration and speed of reading.
Paperback • $7.95 • 135 pages

HYPNOSIS: NEW TOOL IN NURSING PRACTICE
Edited by Gil Boyne, Executive Director, American Council of Hypnotist Examiners
This first-of-its-kind book is a collection of the writings by fourteen registered nurses who successfully use hypnotism in a variety of medical settings. Reveals a new dimension in health care and accelerated healing.
Hardcover • $20.00 • 197 pages

PROFESSIONAL STAGE HYPNOTISM
Ormond McGill
A thorough look at all aspects of entertaining with hypnotism, including showmanship, presentation, staging, securing subjects, and dozens of thrilling routines. Provides a wonderful vista of entertainment which can be performed for all occasions.
Hardcover • $20.00 • 203 pages

HYPNOSPORT
Les Cunningham
An exciting work on the importance of subconscious reprogramming and mental training in athletic performance, Hypnosport is a major contribution to the field of sports conditioning and athletic motivation.
Paperback • $6.95 • 180 pages

SELF HYPNOSIS AND OTHER MIND EXPANDING TECHNIQUES
Charles Tebbetts, Certified Hypnotherapist
A practical and comprehensive guide to the use of self-hypnosis, autosuggestion, and subconscious reprogramming for self-improvement. This new, enlarged edition includes special sections on Weight Control and Stopping Smoking. A best seller.
Paperback • $7.95   Hardcover • $9.95 • 139 pages

STOP SMOKING
Through Self-Hypnosis
Isabel Gilbert
Endorsed by many prominent doctors, Gilbert's simple method uses self-awareness, self-hypnosis, relaxation and self-programming, each taught in a clear, precise and good-humored style. Practical suggestions deal with the temptations of backsliding.
Paperback • $6.95 • 84 pages

THE LEARNING BLOCK
Dean E. Grass, Hypnotherapist
A new method of teaching through mind conditioning that works, developed by an educator who has tested his theories for over thirty years in the classroom. These positive conditioning techniques are useful for both teachers and students.
Paperback • $6.95 • 152 pages

SELECTIVE AWARENESS
Peter Mutke, M.D.
A step-by-step series of easily understood procedures for making contact with and between our various physical and mental parts and functions so we may gain more control over our own health. Includes pain control, accelerated healing, weight reduction, more.
Paperback • $7.95 • 197 pages

SELF-HYPNOSIS and "POWER PROGRAMMING"
Cassettes by Gil Boyne — $9.95 each

#101 SELF-CONFIDENCE THROUGH SELF-IMAGE PROGRAMMING

Radiate dynamic self-confidence; improve your self-image. Overcome the fear of criticism, of rejection, of failure. Feel more lovable and appreciate yourself more.

#102 CONCENTRATION—MEMORY RETENTION—PERFECT RECALL

Liberate your photographic memory! Here is the only scientifically validated memory system known; requires no memorization of key words or word association.

#103 DEEP RELAXATION AND RESTFUL SLUMBER

An incredibly safe and effective technique which enables you to shed the cares of the day and drift off within minutes after your head hits the pillow, and awake refreshed and rejuvenated.

#104 SECRETS OF SUCCESS ATTITUDES

Overcome your subconscious "will to fail" and move rapidly toward your career and financial goals. Begin now to realize the enduring success and wealth that are potentially yours!

#105 WEIGHT CONTROL—TRIM & FIT (specify Men or Women)

This new method conditions your subconscious mind for fast results and gives you a whole new physical-self-image. Changes your eating habits by changing your appetite desires.

#106 SECRETS OF COMMUNICATION AND EXPRESSION

How to present your ideas in a way that ensures acceptance. Speak you absolute confidence and perfect poise—to an audience of hundreds or to a small group or a single person.

#108 DYNAMICS OF SELF-DISCOVERY

Discover the real you! Answers the question, "Who am I?" and creates a powerful belief in your own abilities. Teaches you how to give yourself love, acceptance and approval.

#109 DYNAMIC HEALTH AND RADIANT VITALITY

Overcome fears and negative beliefs about your state of health. You can develop the mental imagery, feeling tone and mental expectancy for vibrant and perfect health.

#114 YOU CAN STOP SMOKING—NOW!

You can overcome the helpless feeling that underlies tobacco addiction! In just a short time, you become free of tobacco—permanently. Enjoy a longer, healthier, happier life.

#115 SEXUAL ENRICHMENT (specify Men or Women)

You have the right to sexual happiness. Powerful desire, total function and glowing fulfillment result from using this breakthrough in sexual therapy. Be all that you can be!

HYPNOSIS TRAINING ON VIDEO

Best seller — Now just $95!
HYPNOTISM TRAINING FILM #501

Gil Boyne —
Teaching and Demonstrating on Video Cassette!
Instantaneous Inductions • Testing and Deepening
Training the Client • Developing Rapid Rapport
Reeducating the Client

Actual live, unrehearsed demonstrations filmed in a classroom setting, using the students in attendance. Includes:
- Five different methods of Instantaneous Induction
- Wolberg Arm Levitation
- Eye Catalepsy, Arm Catalepsy, Automatic Motion, Key Word Reinduction
- Ten methods of deepening the trance
- Post-hypnotic suggestions
- Amnesia and other Hypnotic Phenomena
- Each subject is brought to Somnambulism in minutes

This full-color video training film was the first in the series produced by Westwood Publishing. Boyne demonstrates and simultaneously explains the process in non-technical language.

"The content and quality of training in this film will delight you and satisfy you because:
1. All of the production values are the highest.
2. The video cassette and tape are the highest quality.
3. Most importantly — my reputation depends on it!
For these reasons, I am utterly convinced that you will not only be pleased but thoroughly delighted with your investment in this hypnotism training video."

Gil Boyne

Hypnotism Training Film #501 is available in the following formats:
Two-hour color VHS or Beta video cassette $95.00
Indicate VHS or Beta on order form.

FILL IN AND MAIL ... TODAY

PRIMA PUBLISHING & COMMUNICATIONS
P.O. Box 1260SS
Rocklin, CA 95677

USE YOUR CREDIT CARD AND ORDER BY PHONE
916-624-5718

Qty	Description		Price	Total
		Subtotal		
		Postage & handling		2.50
	In CA add 6% state sales tax	Sales tax		
		TOTAL U.S. funds only		

☐ Check enclosed for $_____ , payable to Prima Publishing

   Charge my ☐ Mastercard ☐ Visa

Account No._____ Exp. Date_____

Signature _____

Your Name_____

Address _____

City/State/Zip _____

Daytime Telephone _____

GUARANTEE
You must be satisfied!
You get a 30-day, 100% money-back guarantee
on all books and audio cassettes
Thank you for your order!